STORY-START MONSTERS

by Franco Pagnucci and Susan Pagnucci

name

Fearon Teacher Aids

Simon & Schuster Supplementary Education Group

Editor: Carol Williams
Copyeditor: Kristin Eclov
Illustration: Susan Pagnucci
Design: Diann Abbott

ISBN 0-86653-999-9

Printed in the United States of America
1. 9 8 7 6 5 4 3 2 1

CONTENTS

INTRODUCTION

"Then there was the bad weather," so begins Ernest Hemingway's *A Moveable Feast,* and what a terrific start it is. Who couldn't write that sentence down and go on from it as though the story were writing itself? Of course, it's in this book that Hemingway tells about the "true sentence." In part two when he talks about having trouble getting a story going, he says to himself, "All you have to do is write one true sentence. Write the truest sentence that you know."

I had known about and been impressed with Hemingway's idea of true sentence starts, but it has only been in the last several years that his idea has become a part of my writing and, more recently, a part of my teaching. It is in starting with a simple fact, a bit of homegrown Yankee wisdom, that a good story sometimes slips out of your pen.

—Franco Pagnucci
poet/college professor

HOW TO USE THIS BOOK . . .

Story Starts

Present the story-start ideas to stimulate students' imaginations. Then provide each child with a copy of the monster front and several monster backs (depending on the length of the story). The monsters have been created with whimsical looks to intrigue children. The spots, the tails, or just the facial expressions may be all that is needed to stimulate story ideas. Or, the independent sentence starts can lead students to stalk stories out of the air, almost magically.

After writing their stories, children can color the monster pages, cut them out, and staple them together. The monster stories can be displayed on a bulletin board to create a monstrous creative-writing center.

Or, rather than cutting out the monster shapes, the pages can be stapled together to make monster booklets. Each child can create an imaginative cover, using a 12" x 18" sheet of construction paper folded in half. The booklet can be filled with several stories.

These whimsical monsters are appropriate to any season or subject. Use them in the classroom, at a library writing lab, or at noon for a "lunch brunch" writing club.

Vocabulary Development

At one time it was thought that "running words by children" (letting them see and hear new words) would increase children's vocabularies. But studies now show that in order for children to learn new words, they must be **taught** the words. Write the words from the "Vocabulary Development" section on the chalkboard during the class writing period. Talk about the words and use them in sentences. The words themselves will generate thoughts and ideas for creative writing.

Additional Activities

Discussions can often extend children's interest on a particular subject. Art projects, cooking ideas, and activities relating to language arts, science, and music are provided so that you can meet these interests. Paint toast, stir up a dirt cake, and try a monster balloon stomp to generate interest and further thought.

ALPHABETARIAN

Story Starts

1. Show children the illustrations in *Alphabrutes* by Dennis Nolan. Each monster makes the sound of a particular letter of the alphabet. Ask children what other sounds they think monsters might make. As a class, figure out ways to phonetically record these sounds on paper. Encourage students to write stories about the strange sounds their monsters utter.
2. Ask students what letter of the alphabet is their favorite. Have children pretend that a monster friend of theirs has a fondness for the same letter. In fact, the monster likes the letter so much, he usually says only words that begin with that letter whenever possible. Invite children to write stories about their alphabet monsters. Encourage them to include the actual monster dialogue in the stories using words that begin with the monster's favorite letter.

Independent Writing

For independent student writing, write this sentence start on the monster front before duplicating. Place the fronts and backs in your classroom writing center.
"'Listen,' he says."

Additional Activity: Language Arts

Read aloud Lark Carrier's *Do Not Touch*. This book is a clever play on words and letters. Invite children to write a book with a similar pattern. Encourage each child to contribute one page to the class book. Design a cover using monsters and letters. Give students an opportunity to check out the class book and take it home to share with family members.

Vocabulary Development

- apprentice
- noise
- recruit
- novice
- words
- aloud
- always
- clamor
- blast
- attention
- tell
- alliteration

Bulletin Board Idea

Cover the background with red paper. Cut out some letters in a variety of styles and sizes using construction paper or wallpaper. Display the letters randomly on the board along with the monster stories. Make black letters for the caption.

name

7

BABYSITTER

Story Starts

1. Invite children to pretend that they are a monster living in the woods. They happen to discover a baby monster who has evidently crawled away from its family. Invite children to write stories telling what they would do with the baby. Ask children how they would care for the baby, what funny things might happen, and how they would go about trying to find the baby's family.
2. Read aloud *Monster and the Baby* by Virginia Mueller. In this story, Monster is trying desperately to stop the baby from crying. Invite children to write a story describing their adventures babysitting a monster. Ask children what they would do if the monster cries, what type of toys they think the baby monster would enjoy, and what they would feed the baby.

Independent Writing

For independent student writing, write this sentence start on the monster front before duplicating. Place the fronts and backs in your classroom writing center.
"No one remembered such heat."

Additional Activity: Puppetry

Children can make puppets using the Babysitter monster on page 9 or any other monster in this book. Cover the writing lines with a piece of white paper before duplicating the monster shape. Give each child a copy of the duplicated monster front and a tongue depressor or pop-sicle stick. Invite students to color the monster with crayons or markers and cut it out. Have students glue the tongue depressor or popsicle stick to the backside of the monster to create a handle on the puppet. Encourage students to write scripts and perform puppet shows for their classmates.

Vocabulary Development

- keeper
- nurse
- woods
- watch
- sitter
- alarm
- fire
- guardian
- spotter
- bodyguard
- protect
- pressure

Bulletin Board Idea

Cover the background with light purple paper. Cut out large safety pin shapes from blue and pink construction paper. Display monster stories and safety pins. Pin a pacifier, clean disposable diaper, empty cereal box, rattle, or other items used by a baby to the board to add interest. Make black letters for the caption.

name

9

10

BRUNCHER

Story Starts

1. Ask children to imagine that their school has organized a fund-raiser breakfast in the park this Saturday. They have been asked to help cook pancakes. They decide to teach the monster who lives next door to flip pancakes and come along on Saturday to help out. Encourage children to write a story about the pancake flipping antics.
2. Ask children what they usually eat for breakfast each morning before coming to school. Ask children what they think a monster would like to have for breakfast. Invite children to write a story about preparing breakfast for a monster before going off to school together.

Independent Writing

For independent student writing, write this sentence start on the monster front before duplicating. Place the fronts and backs in your classroom writing center.
"She sucked on the orange."

Additional Activity: Cooking

Children can paint designs on toast. Mix 1-2 drops of food coloring with 1 tablespoon of milk in jar lids. Provide each small group of students with at least four colors. Children can dip clean paintbrushes into the milky colors and make designs on slices of bread. Toast the bread and serve with butter and honey.

Vocabulary Development

- griddle
- flapjacks
- greed
- stuff
- gorge
- feed
- stew
- sip
- mouthful
- morning
- dawn
- fast

TOASTY STORIES

Bulletin Board Idea

Cover the background with yellow paper. Cut out a toaster shape from gray construction paper. Use a piece of black yarn for the cord and cut a black plug from construction paper. Cut out several slices of toast using brown construction paper. Display the toaster, toast, and monster stories. Decorate the slices of toast with pats of butter, peanut butter, or jam made from pieces of construction paper. Make black letters for the caption.

name

12

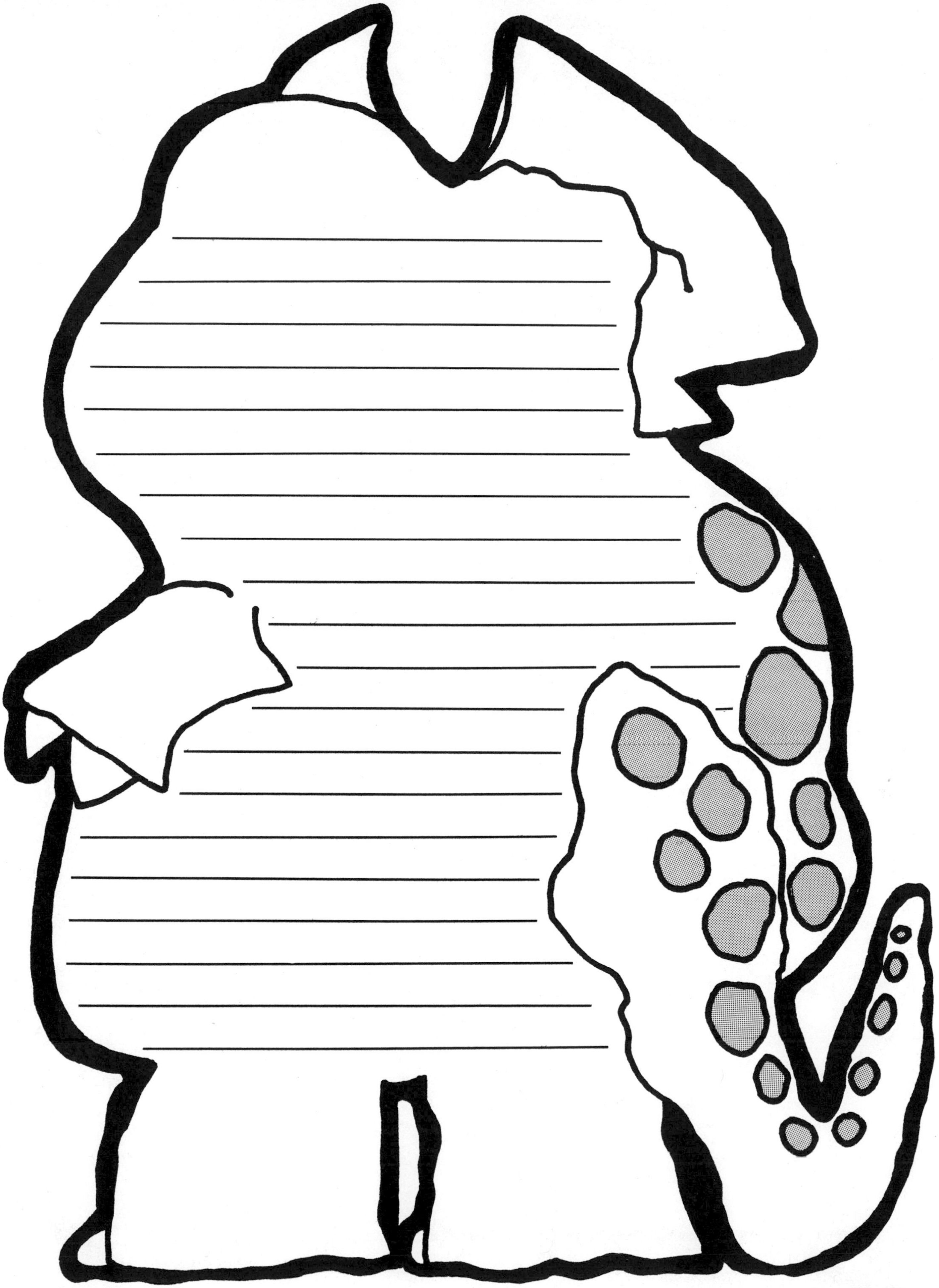

BUNS-AND-CAKES

Story Starts

1. Invite children to pretend that they are a famous chef in a monster restaurant. Ask children what they think their monster patrons would like to eat. Would the monsters spread mayonnaise on their spider sandwiches? Ask children how they would make monster spaghetti. Encourage children to write stories about their monster menus.

2. Read aloud *Mr. Angelo* by Marjory Schwalje. Mr. Angelo cooks whatever he is in the mood for and eats it all day long. If Mr. Angelo is in the mood for fudge, he eats it for breakfast, lunch, and dinner. Problems begin when Mr. Angelo opens a restaurant and bakes an abundance of angel food cakes. Invite students to imagine that they are monsters and have just opened a new restaurant. Encourage students to write stories describing what they are in the mood to eat, what they prepare at their restaurant, and how the patrons react.

Independent Writing

For independent student writing, write this sentence start on the monster front before duplicating. Place the fronts and backs in your classroom writing center.
"Then it was morning."

Additional Activity: Language Arts

Encourage children to participate in a recipe exchange. Ask each student to bring in a copy of their favorite recipe. Combine all the recipes together in a class booklet. As a class, decide how the book will be organized and ask students to categorize the recipes. Give each child a copy of the recipe booklet and encourage each student to design a cover for his or her booklet.

Vocabulary Development

- restaurant
- invent
- lie
- master
- cook
- dawn
- gulp
- swallow
- trick
- boil
- famous
- dinner

COOK UP A STORY

Bulletin Board Idea

Cover the background with green paper. Display monster stories. Make a white construction paper chef hat for each monster. Pin spatulas, potato peelers, or other cooking utensils behind each monster. Make yellow letters for the caption.

name

15

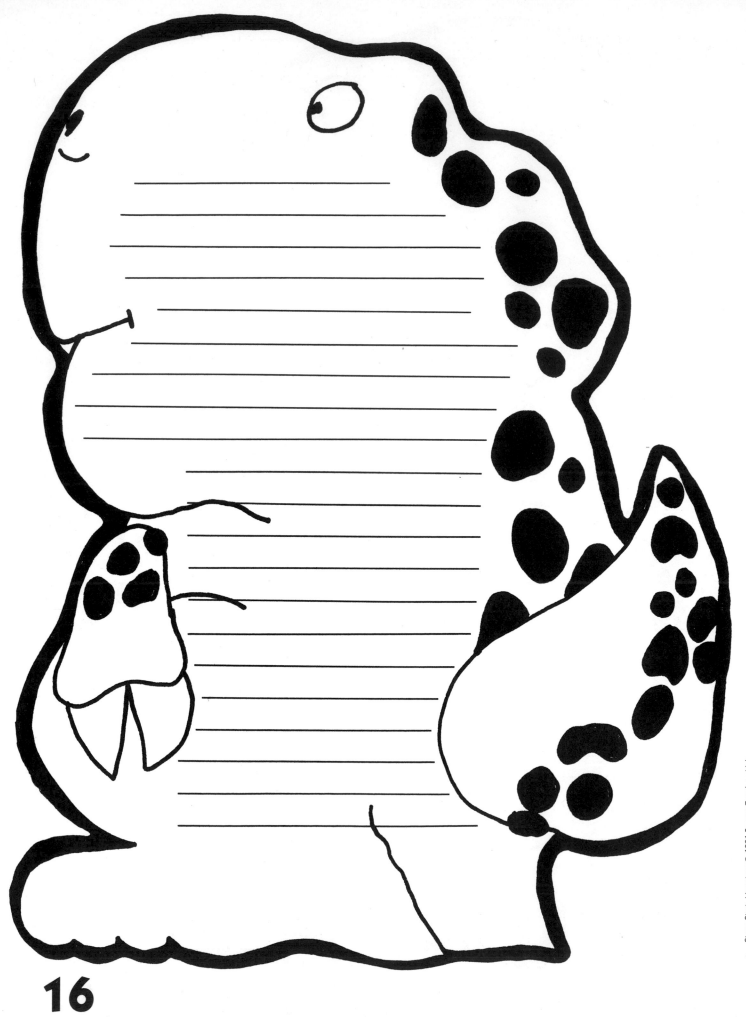

16

DECORATOR

Story Starts

1. Ask children to imagine where a monster might live. In a house? In a cave? In a swamp? Ask children to imagine what a monster's house would look like. Stimulate students to think about how a monster's house and furniture might be different from their homes. For example, would a monster need a specially made chair to accommodate his or her tail when he or she sits down? Would doorways need to be wider? Would a monster need a special bed? Encourage children to write a paragraph describing a monster's house in detail.

2. Ask children to pretend that they have hired an interior decorator to come to their house while their parents are away on vacation. When the decorator shows up, she is a monster with some really wild decorating ideas. Invite children to write a story describing the wild ideas in detail and their parents' reaction to the house's new look when they return home.

Independent Writing

For independent student writing, write this sentence start on the monster front before duplicating. Place the fronts and backs in your classroom writing center.
"The light in the window made him smile."

Additional Activity: Art

Give each child a small piece of tagboard to create a stencil. Students draw a simple design on the tagboard and then cut out the inside of the design to create a shape that can be used for stenciling. Give each child a 12" x 18" sheet of construction paper, paint, and a paintbrush. Instruct students to place the stencil on the construction paper, hold it firmly, and paint across it. Children can then move the stencil to another spot and paint again. The entire page can be filled with stencil designs in a variety of colors.

Vocabulary Development

- painter
- design
- glow
- glass
- fabric
- cave painting
- outline
- tile
- happy
- style
- view
- rearrange

Bulletin Board Idea

Cover the background with several styles of bright wrapping paper. Display the monster stories. Make black letters for the caption.

DECORATOR TALES

name

18

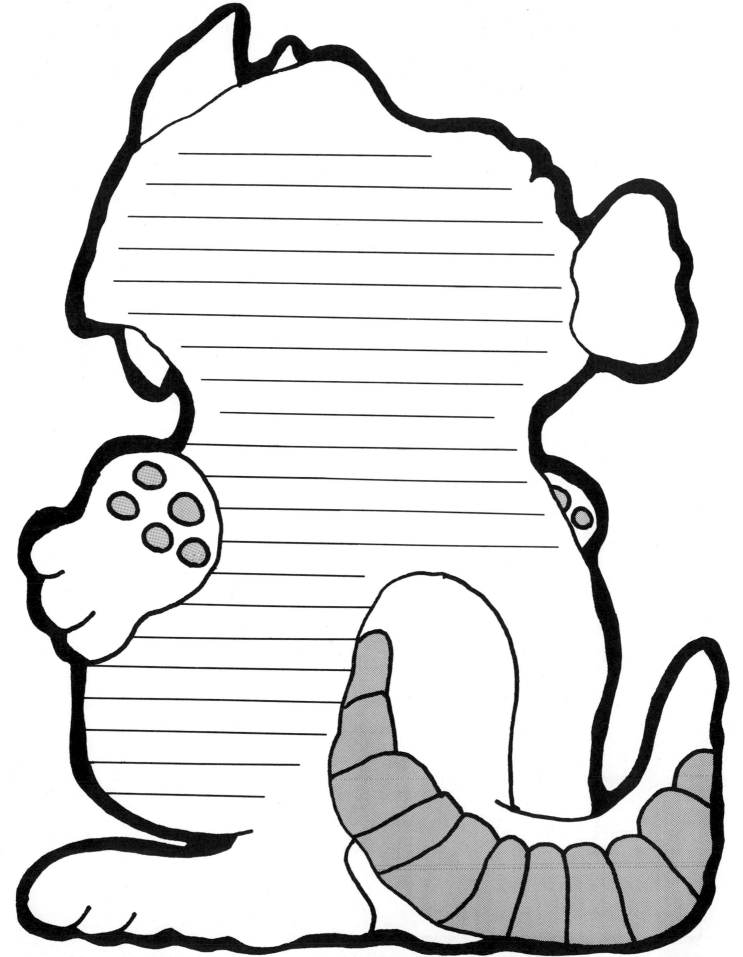

19

FOOTJOKE

Story Starts

1. Read aloud some riddles from *The Monster Riddle Book* by Jane Sarnoff and Reynold Ruffins. Encourage children to create some of their own monster riddles using ideas generated from the riddles in the book. Or, read riddles aloud to students and invite them to write their own answers. Try reading the answers to some of the riddles and invite students to write the questions.

2. Read aloud *How to Prevent Monster Attacks* by Dave Ross. This book provides complete "how to" details for preventing monster attacks. Pass around a clove of garlic for students to smell. Ask children what they think about the old saying that garlic will keep vampires away. Ask children if they think garlic might also keep friends away! Invite students to write stories describing their own inventive ideas for preventing monster attacks.

Independent Writing

For independent student writing, write this sentence start on the monster front before duplicating. Place the fronts and backs in your classroom writing center.
"They had to wait all afternoon."

Additional Activity: Language Arts

Give each child a 2' x 3' piece of cardboard to make a door which will serve as a stage for a joke-hour theatre. Cut two windows at the top of each door. Reproduce two monster fronts from any of the pages in this book for each child. (Remove writing lines before duplicating.) Invite each student to color the two monsters and then glue a tongue depressor or popsicle stick to each to make stick puppets. Encourage students to create original "knock-knock" jokes. Children can poke the head of one monster puppet through a window in their cardboard door and say, "Knock, knock." The second puppet can appear in the other window to say, "Who's there?" and the joke hour begins!

Vocabulary Development

- humor
- laughter
- hilarious
- giggle
- prevention
- expect
- transform
- change
- pretend
- assume
- trick
- guffaw

Bulletin Board Idea

Cover the bulletin board background with blue paper. Make large doors from brown construction paper. Display monster stories in front of closed doors or standing on the threshold of an open door. Make black letters for the caption.

KNOCK, KNOCK--WHO'S THERE ?

name

22

GOSSIPTOOTH

Story Starts

1. Ask children if they have ever known someone who loved to talk. In fact, they loved to talk so much, that it was hard to get them to stop. Invite students to think about problems that might occur if they met a monster with such a gift of gab. Ask children to think of some creative ways to get the monster to stop talking. Review how to correctly use quotation marks before children begin writing their stories.

2. Ask children if they have ever met someone who was very quiet and did not say much at all. Ask children to speculate what reasons people might have for not wanting to talk. Encourage students to create stories in which they meet a baby monster who will not talk. Or, children can write stories about a monster who has a loss of memory and mutters only nonsense.

Independent Writing

For independent student writing, write this sentence start on the monster front before duplicating. Place the fronts and backs in your classroom writing center.
"Afterwards nothing was the same."

Additional Activity: Language Arts

Give each child a 12" x 18" sheet of construction paper to design a poster conveying a monster message. Give each child a copy of one of the monster fronts in this book. (Remove writing lines before duplicating.) Have students glue the monster on their poster and then draw a dialogue bubble above its head. Students may choose to have their monster speak out against drug abuse, smoking, or littering. The monsters can give advice on classroom behavior or library etiquette. Invite students to be creative. Display the finished posters in the classroom or around the school.

Vocabulary Development

- chatter
- mute
- blurt
- mouth
- preach
- spout
- rant
- rattle
- babbler
- magpie
- later
- changed

Bulletin Board Idea

Cover the background with orange paper. Cut white construction paper "word balloons" and display them above each monster story. Each child can carefully print a few words in the balloon above his or her monster. Make red letters for the caption.

name

GREENTHUMB

Story Starts

1. Discuss proper gardening procedures. Ask children if they have ever planted a garden. Invite students to imagine that they are giving gardening lessons to a monster. What would they tell the monster? Encourage children to write stories about the monster's first attempt at planting a garden after receiving their instructions. Invite children to imagine that the monster plants some very unusual looking seeds. What happens when the seeds sprout?

2. Ask students to imagine that they have been working hard on a beautiful garden with a monster friend. They begin to notice that something or someone is eating or stealing all the vegetables. The two of them decide to guard the garden at night to catch the culprit. Invite children to write stories about their detective adventures. What do they discover? What do they do about the problem?

Independent Writing

For independent student writing, write this sentence start on the monster front before duplicating. Place the fronts and backs in your classroom writing center.
"From my bed in the dark, I could hear them."

Additional Activity: Cooking

Give each child a clean flowerpot lined with aluminum foil to make a "dirt cake." Have each child fill his or her pot with a 1/2" layer of crushed chocolate sandwich cookies. Children then fill the pots half full with chocolate pudding, drop in a couple of gummy worms, and then finish filling the pot with pudding. Top with another layer of crushed cookies. Stick a clean, plastic flower in the filled pot. Children can eat their "dirt cakes" using a small, clean plastic spade or shovel.

Vocabulary Development

- garden
- field
- hoe
- watering
- weeds
- spade
- dusk
- alert
- twilight
- rodent
- listener
- greens

TALES TO GROW ON

Bulletin Board Idea

Cover the background with light blue paper. Put a brown strip of construction paper across the bottom to represent the garden. Make carrots using orange and green paper and pin them on the board so the tops just peek up above the garden soil. Fold and crease the leafy green carrot tops to give a 3-D effect. Display monster stories. Make black letters for the caption.

name

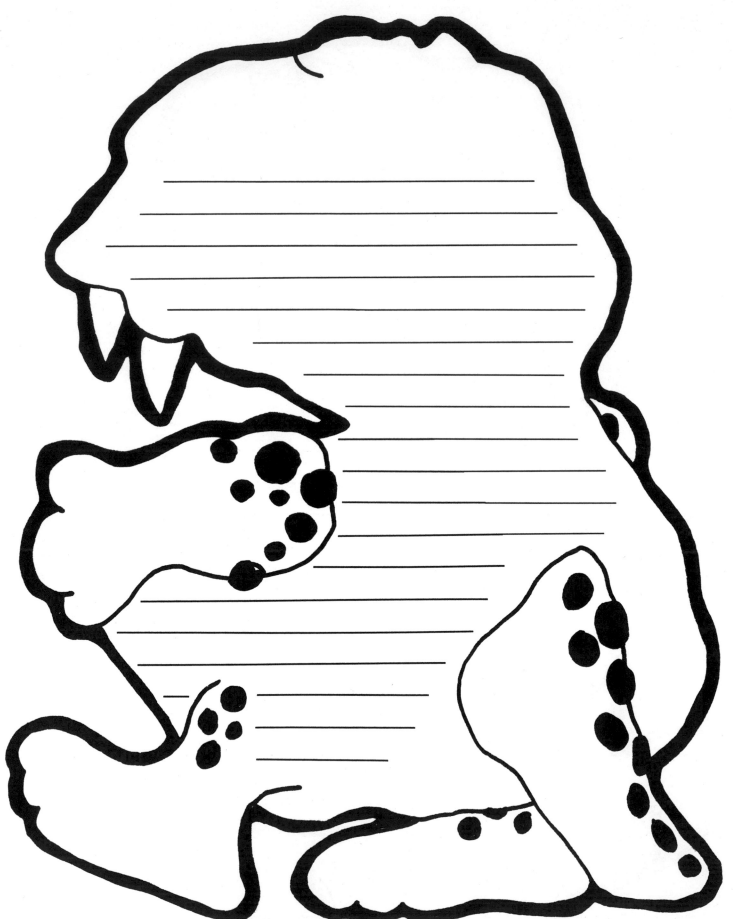

HATCHER

Story Starts

1. Encourage students to imagine that Mrs. Hatcher has just called on the phone and asked them to baby-sit this Friday night. After eagerly accepting the job, they realize that Mrs. Hatcher is a monster. When they arrive at the Hatcher home, Mrs. Hatcher directs them to their charge for the evening—an egg. They are instructed to sit on the huge egg for Mrs. Hatcher while she is away. Ask children how they might react in this situation, how they would get up on the egg, and if it would be comfortable. Invite children to write stories describing the evening's events.

2. Ask students to imagine that upon finding a very large egg in the woods near their home they carefully wrap the egg in a towel and carry it home. On the way home, they notice the egg beginning to crack. By the time they arrive home, a monster has hatched out of the egg. Invite students to write stories about their newly hatched monster. Does it speak English? Is he or she friendly? Is it a secret or do friends and parents know about it? What happens?

Independent Writing

For independent student writing, write this sentence start on the monster front before duplicating. Place the fronts and backs in your classroom writing center.
"I stood up."

Additional Activity: Cooking

Each child can make a noodle nest. In a small saucepan heat 1 can of your favorite frosting until it is liquid. Remove from heat. Stir in 4 cups chow mein noodles and gently mix until coated. Cover each child's desk with a piece of waxed paper. Drop 1/16 of the noodle mixture on each child's waxed paper. Children can use the back of a spoon to make a hollow in the center of the noodle mixture to form a nest shape. Give each child 3-5 jelly beans to put in the nest. Children can share their monster stories with the class and then eat the nests. (Recipe makes about 16 nests.)

Vocabulary Development

- nest
- hatch
- crack
- eggshell
- decided
- sit
- climb
- resist
- fun
- sticks
- speckled eggs
- leaves

Bulletin Board Idea

Cover the background with green paper. Cut large eggs from manilla construction paper and clumps of grass from green construction paper. Display monster stories, eggs, and clumps of grass. Make black letters for the caption.

HATCH A STORY

name

30

31

LUNCHBOX

Story Starts

1. Read aloud *The Hungry Thing* by Jan Slepian and Ann Seidler. The monster in the story mixes up the beginning sounds of words. Before finishing the story, stop and ask students to predict what they think the monster is requesting. Invite students to write stories describing what their monsters would like for lunch in mixed-up word fashion.

2. Read aloud *Bread and Jam for Frances* by Russell Hoban. Frances prefers eating bread and jam and is unwilling to try new foods. Her classmate named Albert always has a very interesting lunch packed with new foods. Ask children what kinds of foods they like to eat for lunch. Invite children to imagine what a monster would like in his or her lunch and write stories about the delicacies.

Independent Writing

For independent student writing, write this sentence start on the monster front before duplicating. Place the fronts and backs in your classroom writing center.

"At lunchtime they were pretending nothing had happened."

Additional Activity: Cooking

"Ting-a-lings" are a great finger food that children can make and enjoy. Assign each student to provide one portion of the recipe ingredients:

2 (6 oz.) pkgs. semi-sweet chocolate chips
4 cups whole-wheat flake cereal
waxed paper

Melt the chocolate chips in a double boiler. Gently mix in the cereal flakes. Drop by tablespoons onto waxed paper. Cool in refrigerator for about 2 hours. Try substituting peanut butter chips, white chocolate chips, milk chocolate chips, or butterscotch chips for the semi-sweet chips. (Makes about 42 clusters.)

Vocabulary Development

- hunger
- bites
- snare
- smells
- surprise
- act
- stomach
- swallows
- upset
- delicious
- trick

Bulletin Board Idea

Cover the background with pink paper. Display monster stories. Pin a paper lunch sack to several monsters. Fill the lunch sacks with lightweight objects, such as empty cereal boxes, empty glue bottles, feathers, or anything else a monster might enjoy eating! Make black letters for the caption.

LUNCH BUNCH

name

34

MASKMAKER

Story Starts

1. Read aloud Virginia Mueller's *A Halloween Mask for Monster.* In Monster's search for the perfect Halloween costume, he tries on several masks, including a mask of a boy, a girl, and a dog. Ironically, these masks are too scary for Monster. Invite students to write stories describing other things that seem so ordinary to us, but might be scary to a monster.
2. Ask children if they have ever been to a costume party. Discuss different types of costumes and ask children what they would like to go dressed as. Encourage children to think about what a monster might like to dress up as. Invite students to write stories about a monster costume party. What were the costumes like? What games did the monsters play? What treats did the monsters have at the party?

Independent Writing

For independent student writing, write this sentence start on the monster front before duplicating. Place the fronts and backs in your classroom writing center.
"Suddenly a wind was in the room."

Additional Activity: Art

Give each child a large paper grocery bag to make a wig. Have children trim the top of the bag so that it rests comfortably on their shoulders when it is placed over their heads. Next, have children cut a giant upside down U shape out of the front of the bag so their faces are exposed. The children can clip and curl the remaining parts of the paper bag to create a new head of hair. Add construction paper bows and hair clips. Encourage children to model their wigs for the class.

Vocabulary Development

- masks
- disguise
- costume
- surprise
- fury
- makeup
- excitement
- two-faced
- festival
- rush

Bulletin Board Idea

Cover the background with orange paper. Display the monster stories. Pin a few masks or other costume pieces around the monsters. Try pinning up an entire costume and pin several stories on top of the costume. Make black letters for the caption.

name

36

MISSINGPIECES

Story Starts

1. Discuss with students how our bodies might be different from a monster's body. Ask students what they would do if they found some strange looking monster part lying on the ground. Would they try to return it? What if the monster came looking for his missing piece? Read aloud *Thump, Thump, Thump!* by Anne Rockwell. Encourage students to write stories patterned after the book, but creating a new dramatic ending.

2. Ask students to pretend that they are a monster who has fallen asleep on an iceberg. When they wake up, their huge monster tail is stuck fast. They give a mighty yank, but the tail doesn't budge. Encourage students to write stories about their attempts to free themselves. Does a passerby help out? Does the weather warm up and melt the ice? How long are they stuck there?

Independent Writing

For independent student writing, write this sentence start on the monster front before duplicating. Place the fronts and backs in your classroom writing center.
"The early cold surprised us."

Additional Activity: Language Arts

Give each child a 9" x 12" sheet of construction paper to draw a monster footprint that fills the entire page. Using a black crayon, children can color around the outside of the footprint. Inside the print, invite children to write sentences describing the monster who made the print. Stimulate students to use creative adjectives. Children can describe the monster's tail, teeth, eating habits, and habitat.

Vocabulary Development

• knee
• jawbone
• shoulder
• caught
• unprepared
• arrange
• loss
• lose
• shock
• search
• trail
• stun

Bulletin Board Idea

Cover the background with light blue paper. Cut out black construction paper footprints and pin them across the bottom of the board. Display monster stories. Make yellow letters for the caption. Use black vinyl self-adhesive tape to make footprints across the floor of your classroom leading from the doorway up the wall to the bulletin board.

THUMP THUMP

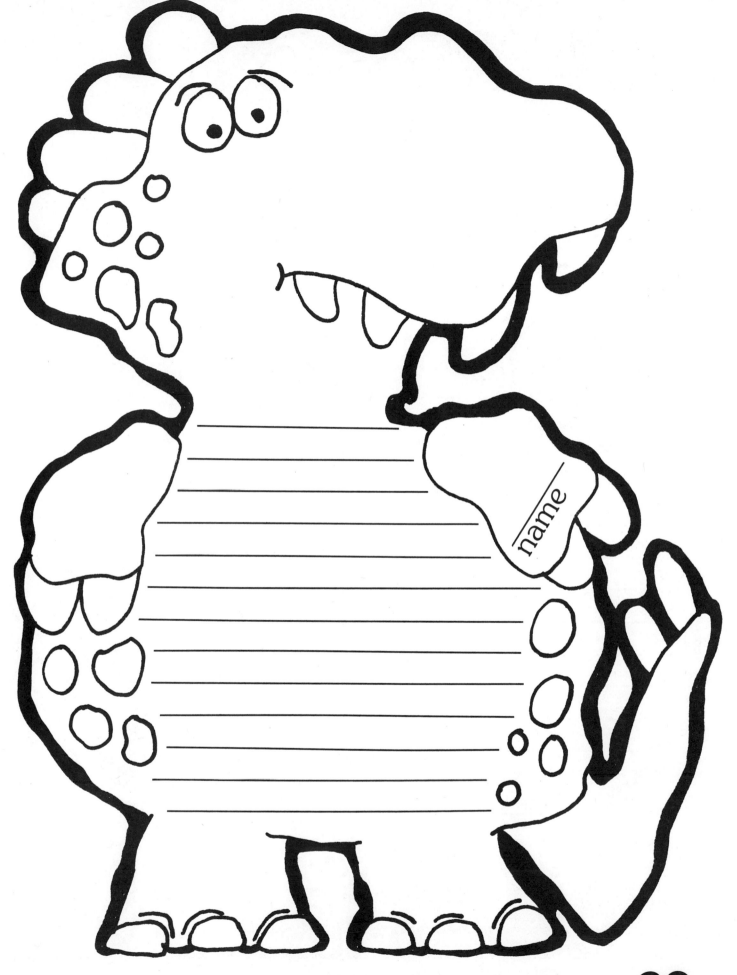

name

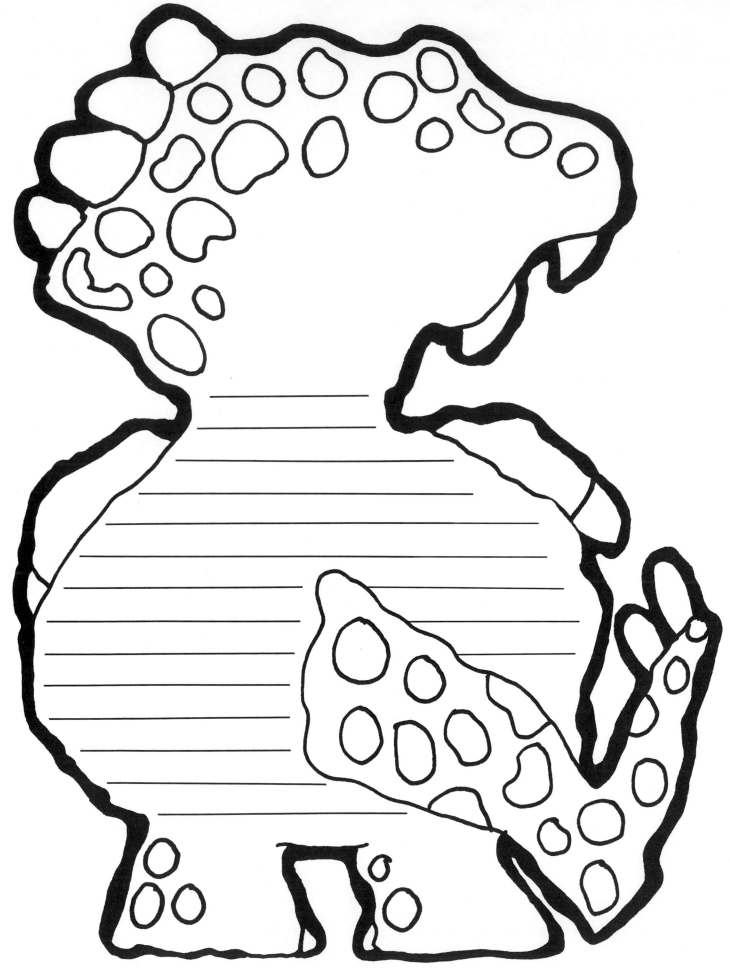

40

ORCHESTRARY

Story Starts

1. Ask children what kind of music they like to listen to. Play samples of various types of music, including country, jazz, classical, opera, and rock. Invite each student to imagine a musical monster that has a fondness for one particular type of music. Encourage children to write stories about their musical monsters. What type of music does the monster like? How does the monster react to other types of music? What happens if the monster cannot listen to music?
2. Invite children to imagine that a monster friend has invited them to join a band. When the monster picks them up to attend the first rehearsal, they notice that the monster is carrying an odd-shaped instrument case. Encourage children to write stories describing the monster's unusual instrument, what the band director says about it, and other important events transpiring at the rehearsal.

Independent Writing

For independent student writing, write this sentence start on the monster front before duplicating. Place the fronts and backs in your classroom writing center.
"The way she stood, I knew something was wrong."

Additional Activity: Music

Create a musical monster band by giving each child a musical instrument to play. Children can make interesting musical sounds using homemade instruments. Sounds can be made by strumming rubberbands that have been stretched tightly across an open shoebox, pounding on an oatmeal box, or blowing on waxed paper wrapped around a comb. Encourage students to move their bodies to the music as well to make the "jam" session an active celebration of sound.

Vocabulary Development

- music
- blare
- boom
- rhythm
- cacophony
- rehearse
- whistle
- march
- direct
- tune
- symphony

Bulletin Board Idea

Cover the background with yellow paper. Use black construction paper to make small radios and headsets. Use black yarn to connect the two earphones to each headset. Display the radios and headsets on the monster stories. Make orange letters for the caption.

HEAR – A – TALE

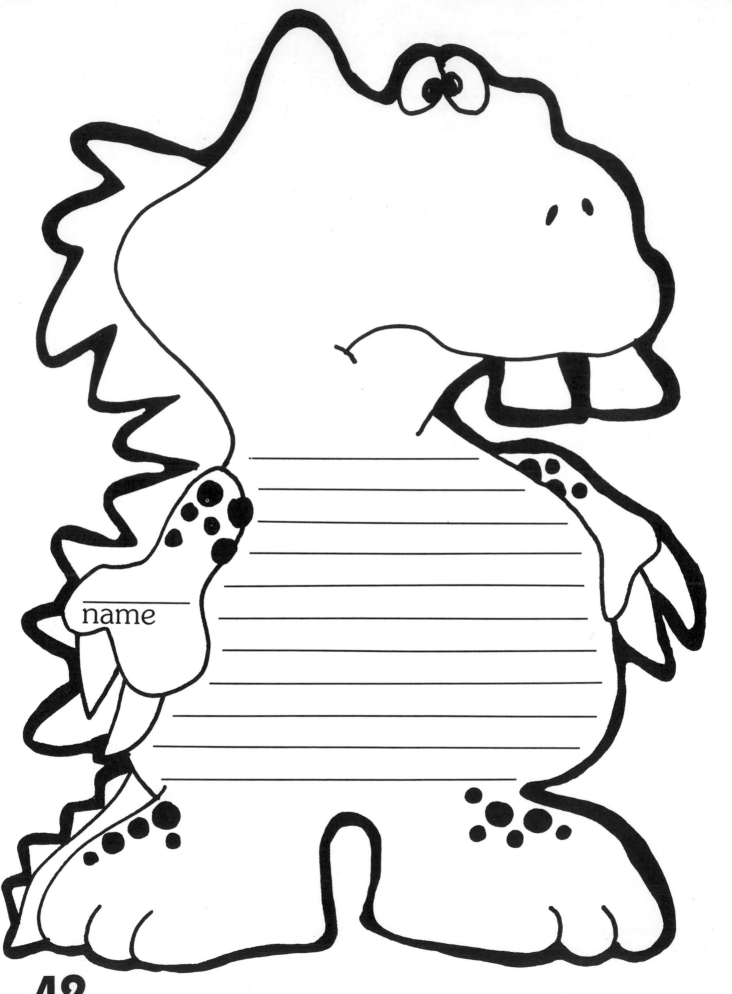

name

42

PARTYBIRD

Story Starts

1. Ask students to imagine that they have been asked to help a group of monsters plan a birthday party for a monster friend of theirs. The monsters have some wild ideas and soon the plans get out of hand. Invite children to write stories about the most outrageous monster party ever. What type of presents did the honored guest receive? What were the party favors? What were the birthday treats? What types of games did the monsters suggest?
2. It is a common custom in the United States to spank a person on his or her birthday and give a "pinch to grow an inch." In Scotland, children are turned upside down and bumped on the head for their birthday. In Japan, it is a custom to give clothes and money as birthday gifts rather than toys. Ask children to write stories describing a special birthday custom for monsters.

Independent Writing

For independent student writing, write this sentence start on the monster front before duplicating. Place the fronts and backs in your classroom writing center.
"The bird chirped once more and then there was silence."

Additional Activity: Game

Give each child a balloon that has been inflated and has a three-inch string tied to it. Have each child use the string to tie the balloon around his or her ankle. When you say "monster stomp" the game begins. Children try to stomp on and pop the balloons on other players' ankles while protecting the balloon on their ankle from popping. When a player's balloon pops, he or she must step out of the play area. The last player with a balloon still attached and inflated is the master monster.

Vocabulary Development

- guests
- party
- nightmare
- terrible
- games
- surprises
- prizes
- racket
- pandemonium
- confusion
- pastry

Bulletin Board Idea

Cover the background with pink paper. Display monster stories. Inflate several small balloons and tie a string to them. Carefully pin the bottom of each inflated balloon to the board and connect the other end of the string to a monster's claw. Add streamers and confetti to the board. Make black letters for the caption.

name

45

RESCUEPUMP

Story Starts

1. Ask students to imagine that they are walking through a field and they notice a large monster who has fallen into an abandoned mining hole. Encourage children to write stories about their attempts to rescue the monster.
2. Encourage children to pretend that their pet monster is "accident-prone." The monster is constantly falling, tripping, and hurting himself or herself. Invite students to imagine their monster in some awkward or unusual situation. For example, the monster may have climbed high up in a tree and and is unable to get down. Ask students to write stories about the rescue efforts and what counsel they might give their monster to prevent such predicaments in the future.

Independent Writing

For independent student writing, write this sentence start on the monster front before duplicating. Place the fronts and backs in your classroom writing center.
"When we stepped onto the road, the rain started."

Additional Activity: Safety

Invite a community volunteer to come to the classroom and present information on dealing with natural disasters such as floods, hurricanes, tornadoes, or earthquakes. Discuss important preventative safety procedures and basic emergency first aid. Compose a list of emergency supplies that would be helpful to have on hand in the classroom or at home. Encourage children to relay the information to their families. A handy flashlight, bottled water, or a quick call to 911 could save a life.

Vocabulary Development

- sinkhole
- shaft
- rescue
- hurricane
- downpour
- save
- rope
- ladder
- aid
- rain
- flash flood
- trap

Bulletin Board Idea

Cover the background with blue paper. Use brown construction paper to make an uneven ground line. Make a hole big enough for several monsters. Cut clumps of grass from green construction paper. Display the monster stories. Make black letters for the caption.

name

48

Story-Start Monsters © 1991 Fearon Teacher Aids

49

SCOTLAND YARDAGE

Story Starts

1. Ask students what excuses they use when they are blamed for something. Ask children if they have ever used the excuse, "A monster must have done it!" Invite students to imagine that a monster overhears them use that excuse one day. The monster then begins actually doing the things he has been blamed for. Encourage students to write stories about the monster's antics.

2. Begin reading aloud Niki Daly's *Joseph's Other Red Sock*. Stop reading the story when Arthur, Harold, and Joseph first pull the monster's tail out of the closet. Invite students to write endings to the story. Encourage children to read their endings aloud for the class. Then read the rest of *Joseph's Other Red Sock*. Children can compare the author's ending with their own.

Independent Writing

For independent student writing, write this sentence start on the monster front before duplicating. Place the fronts and backs in your classroom writing center.
"'What will you say?' I asked her."

Additional Activity: Language Arts

Write the letters of the alphabet across the chalkboard. Assign each letter a number. The letter *A* will be coded as number 1, letter *B* will be number 2, and so on. Write a message to students using the number codes and ask children to decipher it. For example, 8-5-12-12-15 means *hello*. Encourage students to write their own secret messages using the code. Collect the messages and redistribute them so that each student has a message to decode. Provide books from your school or local public library for students interested in more super sleuth ideas, such as disappearing ink.

Vocabulary Development

- search
- explore
- examine
- Sherlock Holmes
- Scotland Yard
- fault
- question
- blame
- "pass the buck"
- explain
- admit
- interrogate

Bulletin Board Idea

Cover the background with yellow paper. Make large question marks and magnifying glasses from black construction paper. Tape plastic wrap over the opening on each magnifying glass. Scatter question marks and magnifying glasses randomly around monster stories. Make red letters for the caption.

WHODUNIT?

name

52

SLEEPER

Story Starts

1. Read aloud *The Dream Eater* by Christian Garrison. Invite children to share some of the dreams they have had recently. Ask children what they do if they have a nightmare and how it makes them feel. Encourage children to write stories about a monster who eats all of their bad dreams and replaces them with pleasant dreams. Have children describe the monster, the dream that they are most grateful that the monster ate, and the good dream that the monster gave to them.

2. Read aloud *Monster Can't Sleep* by Lynn Munsinger. In the story, Monster has trouble falling asleep. His parents try giving him warm milk, reading him a bedtime story, and kissing him good night all to no avail. Ask children if they have ever had trouble falling asleep and what they did to help themselves feel drowsy. Invite children to write stories about a monster who is wide awake at bedtime. Have children include ideas on how to calm the monster and persuade him to drift off to dreamland.

Independent Writing

For independent student writing, write this sentence start on the monster front before duplicating. Place the fronts and backs in your classroom writing center.

"In the morning we looked out and saw the other tent."

Additional Activity: Science/Math

Discuss the importance of sleep. Ask students what time they usually go to bed and what time they get up in the morning. Help children calculate how many hours of sleep they get each night. Make a classroom chart with each student's name on it. Have children record how many hours of sleep they get each night for a week.

Vocabulary Development

- noises
- night
- daylight
- darkness
- sleepless
- count
- trance
- lull
- toss
- awake
- rested

Bulletin Board Idea

Cover the background with deep blue paper. Cut out bright yellow construction paper stars and a moon. Display stars, moon, and monster stories on the board. Pin a small doll blanket or pillow to the bottom of the board. Make white letters for the caption.

BEDTIME TALES

name

54

55

SNIPPER

Story Starts

1. Ask students to pretend they have been asked to design an entire wardrobe for a monster. Ask children to name articles of clothing they would need to design (pants, jacket, vest, scarf, shirt, and so on). Invite children to write stories about their sewing extravaganza. Encourage children to create some intrigue in the story by writing about a problem they have sewing one item of clothing.
2. Read aloud *The Monster and the Tailor* by Paul Galdone. In the story, the Grand Duke offers the tailor a purse full of gold to make him a pair of trousers. But the tailor must sew the trousers while sitting in the graveyard at night. Encourage children to rewrite their own adaptation of the story casting themselves in the role of the tailor.

Independent Writing

For independent student writing, write this sentence start on the monster front before duplicating. Place the fronts and backs in your classroom writing center.
"'No, we can't,' they said."

Additional Activity: Art

Children can make monster mobiles using a variety of textured materials, such as string, tissue, feathers, buttons, and so on. Have each child draw a monster outline on a sheet of drawing paper. Give each child a piece of waxed paper to place over the drawing and spread newspapers beneath the monster. Give children a paper cup filled with a mixture of equal parts of glue and water. Have children dip a piece of yarn in the glue mixture and place it on the waxed paper over the outline of the monster underneath. Invite children to dip the textured materials into the glue and place them on the waxed paper inside the monster outline. Let the projects dry and then peel the monster collage away from the waxed paper. Hang the monster collages with yarn to create unique mobiles.

Vocabulary Development

- tailor
- stitch
- needle
- thimble
- sewing
- disaster
- scissors
- buttons
- woolens
- refuse
- sew
- thread

TAILOR-MADE STORIES

Bulletin Board Idea

Cover the background with bright green paper. Cut several spools from brown construction paper and wrap each with a different color of thick yarn. Cut a large pair of scissors from black and silver paper. Connect the scissors with a brad fastener. Display monster stories, spools, and scissors. Make black letters for the caption.

name

58

STAGEFOOT

Story Starts

1. Ask students to imagine that they have been chosen as the director for a play. The unique aspect of this opportunity is that all of the actors are monsters. Invite students to write stories about their adventures. What play will the monsters perform? Do the monsters show up for rehearsals? How do they look in makeup? What happens on opening night?

2. Read aloud *Where the Wild Things Are* by Maurice Sendak. In the story, Max imagines that he sails off to the land of the wild things and becomes the king. Divide the class into several small groups and ask each group to recreate the story as an opera. Each character must sing his or her part. Invite students to design wild costumes and creative dialogue. Encourage groups to share their performances with the class.

Independent Writing

For independent student writing, write this sentence start on the monster front before duplicating. Place the fronts and backs in your classroom writing center.

"'It was odd,' she said, 'how it all ended.'"

Additional Activity: Cooking

In *Where the Wild Things Are,* Max returned from his imaginary trip because he was lonely and he smelled good things to eat. Ask children what they think Max had for supper that night. Make Peanut Butter Pizza with the class. Make and bake your favorite homemade or packaged pizza crust. Invite students to spread the crust with peanut butter mixed with honey. Students can top the pizza with raisins, banana slices, walnuts, pineapple chunks, or coconut. Cut and serve.

Vocabulary Development

- character
- scenery
- actor
- script
- stage
- props
- director
- lights
- action
- riddle
- mystery
- audience

Bulletin Board Idea

Cover the background with yellow paper. Pin a brown strip of construction paper across the bottom to represent a stage floor. Accordion-fold purple construction paper to make a scrim across the top and curtains on each side. Display monster stories. Make black letters for the caption.

name

61

TIMEOUT

Story Starts

1. Discuss the importance of time as it relates to schedules, appointments, and plans. Ask children what might happen if a bus driver had no regard for time. How would the people who planned to ride the bus feel? Ask children to think of other scenarios where time is of extreme importance. Invite children to pretend that they are a monster who has no regard for time. Encourage children to write stories in which this monster has trouble because he or she is not reliable.

2. Ask students to pretend that they have a watch that runs too fast and they take it to a monster to have it repaired. The monster is able to slow the watch down, but also inadvertently causes the watch to go backwards. Have students imagine that they are standing beside the monster staring at the watch tick in the wrong direction while it starts transporting them back in time. Invite students to write stories about their travels back in time.

Independent Writing

For independent student writing, write this sentence start on the monster front before duplicating. Place the fronts and backs in your classroom writing center.
"Looking back on it, I guess you were right."

Additional Activity: Language Arts

Use small strips of paper to write "time messages" to your students, such as "You may get a drink at 11:05" or "You may go to morning recess 4 minutes early." Write one message for each student and individually wrap each message in aluminum foil. Place each message in the bottom of a cupcake paper. Fill each cupcake paper with cake batter and bake. Frost the cupcakes and serve them with milk in the morning. You'll have giggles all day as students carry out their time messages.

Vocabulary Development

- clock
- alarm
- souvenir
- flashback
- timepiece
- grandfather clock
- hourglass
- remember
- yesterday
- past
- then
- now

Bulletin Board Idea

Cover the background with orange paper. Cut a large stopwatch from white construction paper and add gold details. Use a black marker to add numbers and hands to the watch. Display the large stopwatch in the center of the board with the monster stories around it. Make black letters for the caption.

64

_____
_____
_____
_____
_____
_____
_____
_____
_____
_____

name _____